Opening Your Third Eye

Macrobiotics and Spirituality

EDWARD ESKO

My view is that this gland is the principal seat of the soul, and the place in which all our thoughts are formed. The reason I believe this is that I cannot find any part of the brain, except this, which is not double. Since we see only one thing with two eyes, and hear only one voice with two ears, and in short have never more than one thought at a time, it must necessarily be the case that the impressions which enter by the two eyes or by the two ears, and so on, unite with each other in some part of the body before being considered by the soul. —Rene Descartes

Opening Your Third Eye
Macrobiotics and Spirituality

Contents

Opening Your Third Eye: Macrobiotics and Spirituality
From a lecture at the Kushi Institute
Illustrations by Naomi Ichikawa
Edited by Noreen Dillman Purcell

Copyright © 2016 Edward Esko
ISBN-13: 978-1537050454
ISBN-10: 1537050451

Published by Amberwaves Press
P.O. Box 487
Becket, MA 01223
Amberwaves.org
Printed in the U.S.A.
First Edition

The Pineal Gland

The third eye is commonly associated with the pineal gland. The pineal gland is somewhat mysterious and not well understood, being located deep within the brain. From antiquity, the pineal gland was considered to have mystical, spiritual, and religious associations. Before we look at those aspects, let's discuss some facts about the pineal gland.

1. The pineal gland is a small gland at the center of the brain with the shape and appearance of a tiny pinecone. It has been associated with pinecone imagery throughout history.
2. The pineal gland is the only unpaired structure within the brain. All of the other structures are divided into two: left and right hemispheres, right side, left side. The pineal gland is unified and not divided. It is about 5 to 8 millimeters in length, about the length of a grain of rice.
3. Unlike the rest of the brain, the pineal is not isolated from the circulatory system by the blood-brain barrier that protects the brain. Instead the pineal receives a profuse supply of blood, second only to the kidneys. The kidneys receive the largest blood supply; about one-third of the heart's output because of their filtering and purifying function. This tiny gland receives the second largest blood supply. Is that not strange?
4. The pineal gland contains rods and cones, which in the retina are photo (light) receptors, making it

highly sensitive to light. The pineal is located deep within the brain, so the presence of light receptors seems strange.

5. The pineal gland secretes melatonin. Melatonin regulates the sleep-wake cycle in response to light and darkness.

6. On scans of the brain, the pineal gland often shows signs of calcification, even as early as two years old. By age seventeen, it is estimated that 40% of Americans have a calcified pineal gland. The incidence of calcification increases as people age.

7. There is evidence that the pineal gland regulates the function of the pituitary gland, including the regulation of hormones involved in ovulation, menstruation, and sexual function. The pituitary is often called the "master" gland.

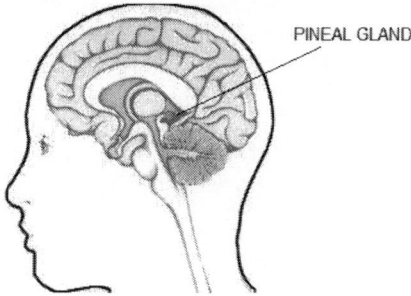

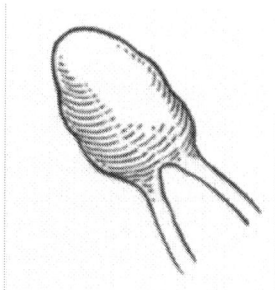

PINEAL GLAND

The Sleep-Wake Cycle

Melatonin promotes drowsiness and sleep. The production of melatonin peaks before puberty. It declines as we age. Kids are producing melatonin and can easily fall asleep. Melatonin inhibits the development of sex characteristics. It declines just before puberty and with that decline, sex characteristics begin to develop. Production of melatonin occurs in response to the presence or absence of light. Sunlight during the day makes the production level decline. At night, with darkness, production increases. In my view, melatonin is a more yin, calming and relaxing substance in comparison to a hormone such as adrenaline, which is activating and stimulating or more yang.

Pinecone Imagery

Pinecone imagery dates back to the dawn of recorded history. In the image shown below, from ancient Egypt, we see figures holding pinecones in a field of light, offering them to the light. Similar images go back to ancient Sumer, depicting the special nature of the pinecone that many believe to be a symbol of the pineal gland. In Buddhism and Hinduism pinecone depictions exist, as do markings corresponding to the pineal gland. On the forehead of Indian gods and saints, we see a mark corresponding to the third eye. To this day, women in India place a mark, known as a *bindi*, between their eyebrows. Many Buddha icons feature marks or spirals in the third eye region. Buddha statues are depicted wearing hats that resemble pinecones. The towers at Angkor Wat in Cambodia also resemble pinecones.

In Christianity, symbolized by the Vatican, there is a mysterious statue of a pinecone in Vatican City (see below.) The birds on either side of the statue are similar to Egyptian bird icons, leading to speculation that the statue made its way to the Vatican from Egypt. The Pope sometimes carries a staff with a pinecone carving on its top. Also, the high hat worn by the Pontiff often has a mark in the center that represents the third eye. Pinecone imagery has been a feature of religious art from the beginning of recorded history. You can Google "pinecone imagery," "pineal gland," or "third eye" to see many examples.

The Chakras

In order to understand the pineal gland, we need to consider the understanding of chakras. What are the chakras? They are highly charged centers of energy. How do they arise? What is their origin? The chakras are channeling and concentrating the energy of the universe itself, from the cosmos down to the planet, and from the planet back out to the cosmos. In macrobiotics, we call the incoming cosmic force "heaven's force." We call the energy that radiates back out "earth's force." Heaven's force is comprised of incoming light, radiation, particles, cosmic rays, meteorites, and other forms of visible and invisible energy.

These yang (downward) and yin (upward) energies form a central core of energy deep within the body. The seven chakras arise along this central line. This core is where our life energy is strongest. Our vital functions arise along this line, such as heartbeat, absorption of nutrients, and consciousness. As we move away from the central core toward the periphery of the body, life energy becomes less. We can live without an arm or a leg, but we cannot live without these core functions.

The pineal gland is located in the midbrain chakra, which counting from the lowest chakra is the sixth chakra. This area of the brain is highly yang or contracted, so much so that the pineal gland is not divided into left and right, but is fused into one unit.

Crown

7

6 3rd Eye

5 Throat

4 Heart

3 Solar

2 Sacral

Root

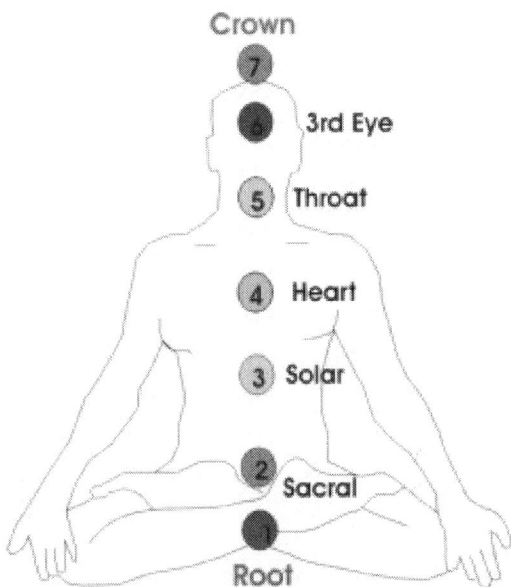

Energy from the cosmos spirals into the top of the head, at the seventh or crown chakra. It flows downward and charges the pineal gland. From there it continues downward, creating the uvula. Energy streaming up from the earth charges the tongue. The mouth is thus highly charged by heaven and earth. On both sides of the uvula are the salivary glands, also highly charged by cosmic energy. Thus, saliva is highly energized. That is why chewing energizes and actively breaks our food down into smaller and smaller particles.

Two Types of Vision

The work on the circulation of the light depends entirely on the backward-flowing movement, so that the thoughts (the place of heavenly consciousness, the heavenly heart) are gathered together. The heavenly heart lies between the sun and moon (the two eyes.) —The Secret of the Golden Flower (T'ai I Chin Hua Tsung Chih)

What is taking place in the pineal gland? As we saw, the pineal gland contains photo- sensitive rods and cones. What type of vision is taking place there? There obviously is a gathering of vibration from the cosmos in toward the midbrain and pineal gland. That is the more yang, incoming, or centripetal dimension. From the external cosmos, light and other forms of vibration come in. The eyes detect that light. That movement occurs in the form of a yang, centripetal spiral. But the pineal gland, with its rods and cones, not only has energy coming in, but also is actually looking out. Looking out into what world? The pineal is the gateway into the spiritual universe.

Vibration is coming in to our physical eyes from the universe and converging at the yang midbrain and pineal gland. What is the form of our universe? Ultimately what? Vibration converging toward the earth becomes increasingly dense, physical, and material. Third eye vision is moving away from matter and toward non-physical vibration that cannot be perceived through our senses. Our vision in the physical world is created by light converging at the midbrain where it is processed as vision.

Third eye vision is seeing the other way, looking out at the centrifugal universe that is moving away from us. Through the pineal gland, we are able to glimpse that universe which is not visible to the eye.

Incoming Vision	**Outgoing Vision**
Centripetal (yang)	Centrifugal (yin)
Spiraling in	Spiraling out
From the physical universe	Toward the vibrational universe
Vibration toward matter	Matter toward vibration
Physical and material	Spiritual and vibrational
Past	Future
Fruit	Seed
Physical eyes	Third or spiritual eye
Sensory perception	Non-sensory perception
Infinity into yin and yang	Yin and yang into infinity

When we see the physical universe we are actually seeing the past. When you look up into the night sky, for example at the Andromeda galaxy, which is the galaxy closest to earth, you are seeing light that left Andromeda 2.5 million of years ago. Light reaching earth from the sun is actually 8 minutes and 20 seconds old; that from the moon is about 1.3 seconds old. Looking at anything in our material world means we are actually seeing the past. The physical universe is the world from which we came. The vibrational universe, perceived by the third eye, is the world toward which we are going. The pineal gland represents the fruit of the material universe, while at the same time; it is the seed of our future spiritual universe.

Our physical world is the result of the absolute oneness of infinity, endlessly dividing into two, or yin and yang. The spiritual world is the opposite. It is the relative, endlessly dividing world of yin and yang, returning toward the absolute oneness of infinity. These two worlds are completely opposite from one another. The first world is perceived through the physical eyes, the second, by the third or spiritual eye.

A Disciplined Approach

Some people are confusing the gradual opening of the pineal gland through disciplined meditation and training with the attempt to gain instant enlightenment through the use of hallucinogenic plants. Many people, including celebrities, have experimented with the tropical plant known as *ayahuascha.* Some have journeyed to the Amazon to participate in ceremonies that feature a tea made with this indigenous plant.

Ayahuascha contains a hallucinatory substance known as DMT. It is a tropical equatorial plant. Like other hallucinogens, such as LSD, mescaline, and peyote, it is extremely yin, with the potential to be severely damaging to one's health and mental balance. Rather than the gradual awareness of peaceful spiritual light that follows mediation training, participants in ayahuascha ceremonies often see terrifying visions of darkness and misery, alternating back and forth between darkness and brightness, with the appearance of horrifying creatures and otherworldly beings. They need to be aware that these hallucinations are the product of their own conscious and subconscious mind, including the mental limitations caused by past extreme foods, especially animal foods, as well as the sudden violent discharge of past extremes, and not a vision of the vibrational worlds as they truly exist. One indication of the extreme nature of ayahuascha is its horrible taste, the common experience of violent nausea (the body seems to be instinctively rejecting it), and the diarrhea that follow its ingestion.

Having lived through the 1960s, the ayahuascha fad reminds me of the LSD craze that swept through my generation. At that time, Michio Kushi warned of the danger of confusing the hallucinatory experience of LSD and similar drugs with the genuine quest for health and spirituality. In a lecture entitled, "Psychedelics and the Way of Eating," published in the *Order of the Universe*, July 1967, he stated:

"The difference between our attitude towards time and that of people using drugs is a good indication of the distance between us. We teach the necessity of taking time, which is yang, in cooking, in learning, in development, and in life in general. When we choose vegetables to eat, we pick those that have grown slowly, suffering cold and rugged terrain, over the expanded products of southern climates that grow quickly. Those who take drugs are looking for an instantaneous way to enlightenment. In this way they are very similar to our materialistic society that promotes instant gratification. Their growth is always like the tropical plants they use to achieve this—quick, beautiful, and luxurious for a while, but finally unstable and quick to fall. Those who use drugs do so in order to be 'high,' but this is not what we want. Our aim is to *broaden* and *deepen* our understanding until it can include infinity itself."

Harmful Foods

Let us now study the practical steps we can use to train, condition, and gradually open the third eye. Our goal is to stop and reverse the calcification of the pineal gland; or in other words, to stop the process of calcification and dissolve the calcification that exists.

The composition of these calcified deposits offers a clue as to their origin. They contain, in addition to calcium, substances such as fluoride, phosphorus, mercury, and other heavy metals. The origin of these elements is the foods we eat and the water we drink. Perhaps the number one source of calcification in the body is milk and other dairy foods. That may explain the incidence of calcification in two-year old children. Children with this condition were most likely fed cow's milk formula rather than being breastfed. I would assume calcification of the pineal gland is rare in breastfed infants. The first step in stopping the calcification of the pineal gland is to stop consuming milk and dairy products.

What else in the modern diet causes calcification? Red meat. Meat also leads to osteoporosis. Meat-eating populations tend to have the highest rates of osteoporosis. The breakdown of animal protein leads to a strong acid condition in the body. These strong acids block the absorption of calcium and leach calcium from the bones. The bones become hollow and porous. Leached or unabsorbed calcium circulates in the bloodstream. The pineal receives a heavy supply of blood, and so is a frequent site for calcium deposition, as are the kidneys.

Refined sugar creates a strong acid condition in the body that leaches calcium from bones and teeth, leading to the deposition of calcium as described above. The phosphorous in these deposits most likely comes from cola drinks. That may explain the estimated 40% rate of calcification occurring in the pineal gland by age seventeen. A high sugar, high soft drink diet leads to the ongoing cycle of decalcification-re-calcification that affects the pineal gland.

Fluoridated water adds to toxic accumulation in the pineal gland. Water quality is a big headache today. It is better to avoid fluoridated or chemically treated water, by using spring, well, or filtered water. Fluoride is also added to toothpaste today. To avoid this, use fluoride-free toothpaste.

The Unique Role of Brown Rice

The first step in establishing pineal health is to avoid the foods and substances mentioned in the previous section. The second step is to adopt a plant-based macrobiotic diet that avoids meat, dairy, and sugar. There is a large secret within the macrobiotic diet that very few understand. Recall the unique structure of the pineal gland. As Rene Descartes understood, the pineal gland is the only structure in the brain that is unified and not divided into left and right. Compared to divided structures, this unified structure is highly yang or contracted.

If you examine grains, beans and seeds closely, you will see a division or split between left and right. Beans are divided, seeds are divided, and grains such as barley, millet, and wheat are all divided. The only grain that is not split or divided, but completely unified is brown rice. It is no wonder that countries and regions of the world that ate brown rice developed the arts of meditation and unified spirituality.

Brown rice, especially short grain brown rice, is unified. Because of that, short grain brown rice is the central food for toning and conditioning the pineal gland. Eating brown rice on a daily basis and chewing it well heals and strengthens the pineal gland. Aside from being eaten daily, brown rice can also be applied externally to activate the pineal gland. Michio Kushi introduced this method many years ago.

A grain of rice can be applied to a specific acupuncture point to activate the meridians and organs that correspond to it. However, it is difficult to keep the grain in place, so Michio suggested that we tape it to the point. We can apply this technique to activate the pineal gland by taping a grain of rice on the forehead, to the point that corresponds to the pineal gland. That point is generally in the location of the bindi in the center of the forehead between and slightly above the eyebrows. The taped rice can be left on for several hours or overnight.

All foods are energy and project an aura. The aura of brown rice and other cereal grains is golden white. Rice growing in the field displays a golden aura that you can see from a distance. That golden color matches the inner golden light that becomes visible when you open the third eye.

Foods that Cleanse

Foods such as miso and sea vegetables detoxify the body; they help the body discharge heavy metals and other toxins. They also cleanse the pineal gland. Cooked leafy greens also help loosen and dissolve hardness in the body, including discharging excess calcium from the pineal gland. Fresh chopped scallion can be used daily as garnish for the same purpose. Brown rice vinegar can also aid in this process.

There are several foods in the macrobiotic diet that have what I refer to as "melting" or "softening" effects. Daikon radish is one of these foods. One way to prepare it is to slice it into thick rounds, bring it to a boil, and simmer it covered for 40 minutes or more until it becomes fork tender and practically melts in your mouth. It can be seasoned with shoyu or with miso gravy. We refer to this dish as "daikon steak." Daikon can also be eaten in the dried form or sometimes grated raw. Like daikon, dried shiitake mushroom and unpasteurized sauerkraut also have a "melting" or "softening" effect on the body.

Certain berries resemble the pineal gland. Raspberries and blackberries are examples. They have a sweet and sour taste. Enjoyed in season, they make the pineal gland soft and flexible. Brown rice, on the other hand, has a toning and strengthening effect.

Some evidence has been found that the element iodine blocks the uptake of calcium by the pineal gland. Sea vegetables provide a good source of iodine in the diet. Sea vegetables can be used in soups and side dishes, and are especially good as daily condiments. I especially recommend the dulse and other sea vegetable powders produced in Maine. They are available at most natural food stores. A teaspoonful of sea vegetable condiment can be sprinkled daily on brown rice and other foods.

Vibrational Healing

"The Book of the Yellow Castle says: 'In the square inch field of the square foot house, life can be regulated.' The square foot house is the face. The square inch field in the face: what could that be other than the heavenly heart? In the middle of the square inch dwells the splendor. In the purple hall of the city of jade dwells the God of Utmost Emptiness and Life. The Confucians call it the center of emptiness; the Buddhist, the terrace of living; the Taoists, the ancestral land, or the yellow castle, or the dark pass, or the space of former heaven. The heavenly heart is like the dwelling place, the light is the master." —The Secret of the Golden Flower (T'ai I Chin Hua Tsung Chih)

Together with a balanced macrobiotic diet, we can also activate and heal the pineal gland by using the direct application of vibration or energy. Ancient people understood that different sounds vibrated at different frequencies and activated certain organs or regions of the body. Sounds can be understood in terms of yin and yang. Certain sounds are open and expansive, or more yin. Opposite sounds are closed and contractive, or more yang. A sound such as "A," pronounced "Ah," is open and expanded. It is used to depict large concepts, including religious and spiritual concepts. In English, the word "God" is built on its sound, as are corresponding names such as "Allah," "Brahman," "Ammon," and "Yahweh."

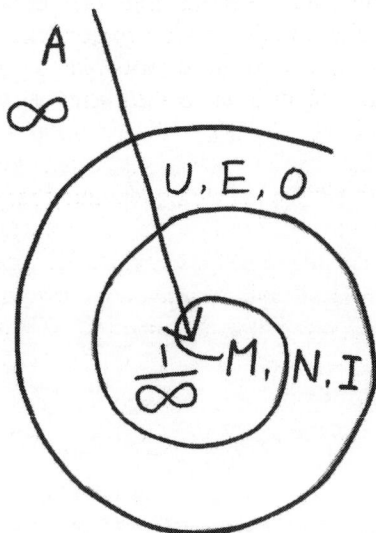

Illustration by Naomi Ichikawa

How about sounds such as "Mm," "Nn," or "I" (pronounced "Eee.") These sounds are more yang or contracted. They represent the individual and not the universal. Rather than "God," we say "me." The words "I, me, mine" are based on these sounds. These more contractive sounds resonate in the compact head, especially the "Mm" sound. The "Ah" sound resonates or vibrates much further down in the body toward the more expanded intestines. The "U" sound (pronounced "Uuu") vibrates the region of the body in between these upper and lower poles, specifically the middle of the chest in the region of the heart.

The three primary sounds "Ah" "U" "Mm" represent the creation of the universe from non-manifested unity or God. "U" is the world of vibration, comprising the entire manifested universe. "Mm" is the tiny manifested world within the universe, including our human world.

Combining these sounds into one continuous chant activates the three major chakra regions of the body. The sound "Aum" is a pure description of the genesis of the universe from the infinite to the infinitesimal, similar to that depicted in the Book of Genesis and other accounts of creation. (This ancient chant is often pronounced as "Om.") The "Ah" sound activates and charges the lower chakras, including the intestinal chakra, while the "U" sound activates the middle chakras, especially the heart chakra. The "Mm" sound activates the midbrain chakra, including the pineal gland. Needless to say, this sound helps energize and loosen stagnated deposits in the pineal gland.

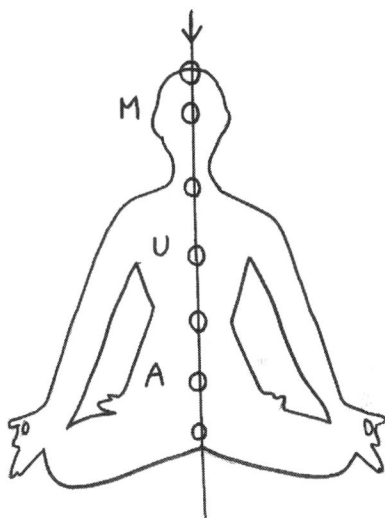

Illustration by Naomi Ichikawa

To practice the Aum chant, sit with a straight posture. Place your hands in your lap, with your left hand on top of your right hand. Touch both thumbs together to make a complete circuit of energy.

Close your eyes and breathe in a quiet and relaxed rhythm. After a minute or two, begin to breathe more deeply, with your breathing centered below the chest in the abdomen. Let your mind relax. After several deep breaths, begin to make the sound of "A-U-M," repeating seven to ten times. When you complete the sound, sit with a quiet or empty mind. Keep your eyes closed, return to normal breathing, and begin to focus your attention inward toward the pineal gland and third eye. In doing that, see if you can begin to glimpse golden light. To complete your meditation, slowly open your eyes and relax.

These simple practices—avoiding harmful foods and water, eating a balanced plant-based diet centered on brown rice and other whole grains, and practicing meditation and chanting on a regular basis—help melt stagnation in the pineal gland. They help open your third eye vision so as to glimpse the endless spiritual world of pure golden light.

Resources

Kushi Institute, 198 Leland Road, Becket MA 01223, 413-623-5741, www.kushiinstitute.org. World Center for Macrobiotic Learning. Programs include the Way to Health Residential Seminar, Macrobiotic Leadership Training, Specialty Workshops, and the annual Kushi Summer Conference. Programs presented by the world's leading macrobiotic teachers and educators. The Kushi Institute sponsors a natural products store with mail order books, CDs, and videos by the author plus a range of high-quality macrobiotic foods. Visit KushiStore.com.

Planetary Health/Amberwaves, PO Box 487, Becket MA 01223, 413-623-0012, www.amberwaves.org. A grassroots network devoted to preserving amber waves of grain and keeping America and the planet beautiful. Amberwaves is publisher of numerous books and a quarterly newsletter with articles by Edward Esko and Alex Jack.

Macrobiotics Today/**George Ohsawa Macrobiotic Foundation (GOMF)**, 1277 Marian Ave., Chico CA 95928, 800-232-2372, www.OhsawaMacrobiotics.com. GOMF is a macrobiotic publisher and educational center on the West Coast. *Macrobiotics Today* quarterly features articles by Edward Esko and other macrobiotic authors.

About the Author

Edward Esko is one of the world's most active contemporary macrobiotic teachers. Over the past four decades, he has lectured and counseled in Europe, Asia, Latin America, and throughout North America, including at the United Nations, and has written and edited numerous books and articles. Building on the teachings of George Ohsawa, Michio Kushi, and other macrobiotic pioneers, he has applied yin and yang—the universal principles of change and harmony—to helping solve issues of personal and planetary health. He has served as Vice President of the East West Foundation. He currently serves as Associate Director and Senior Faculty member at the Kushi Institute. His latest books include *Yin Yang Primer, Contemporary Macrobiotics, Rice Field Essays, Dandelion Essays, Ki: The Energy of Life*, and *The Next Twenty Years*, as well as *Cool Fusion* and *Corking the Nuclear Genie,* coauthored with Alex Jack. Books are available from amazon and KushiStore.com. Contact: edwardesko@gmail.com.

18383507R00018

Printed in Great Britain
by Amazon